Sea
Anemones

by Lola M. Schaefer

Consulting Editor: Gail Saunders-Smith, Ph.D.

Consultant: Jody Byrum, Science Writer,
SeaWorld Education Department

Pebble Books

an imprint of Capstone Press
Mankato, Minnesota

Pebble Books are published by Capstone Press
1710 Roe Crest Drive, North Mankato, Minnesota 56003
www.capstonepub.com

Library of Congress Cataloging-in-Publication Data
Schaefer, Lola M., 1950–
    Sea anemones/ by Lola M. Schaefer.
    p. cm.—(Ocean life)
    Includes bibliographical references (p.23) and index.
    Summary: In simple text and illustrations, describes the sea anemone.
    ISBN-13: 978-0-7368-0248-2 (hardcover)
    ISBN-10: 0-7368-0248-7 (hardcover)
    ISBN-13: 978-0-7368-8219-4 (paperback)
    ISBN-10: 0-7368-8219-7 (paperback)
    1. Sea anemones—Juvenile literature. [1. Sea anemones.] I. Title. II. Series.
    QL377.C7S25 1999
    593.6—dc21   98-46076

Note to Parents and Teachers

The Ocean Life series supports national science standards for units
on the diversity and unity of life. The series shows that animals
have features that help them live in different environments. This
book describes and illustrates sea urchins, their homes, and their
parts. The photographs support early readers in understanding the
text. The repetition of words and phrases helps early readers learn
new words. This book also introduces early readers to subject-
specific vocabulary words, which are defined in the Words to Know
section. Early readers may need assistance to read some words and
to use the Table of Contents, Words to Know, Read More, Internet
Sites, and Index/Word List sections of the book.

Printed in the United States of America in Eau Claire, Wisconsin.
051915   008977R

Table of Contents

Sea anemones are ocean animals.

Some sea anemones attach themselves to coral reefs.

8

Some sea anemones attach themselves to rocks.

10

Sea anemones
can be colorful.

Sea anemones have soft bodies.

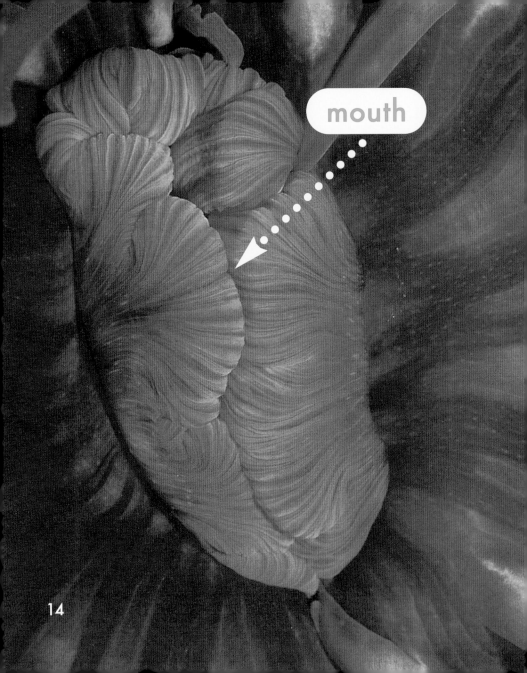

mouth

Sea anemones have
a mouth.

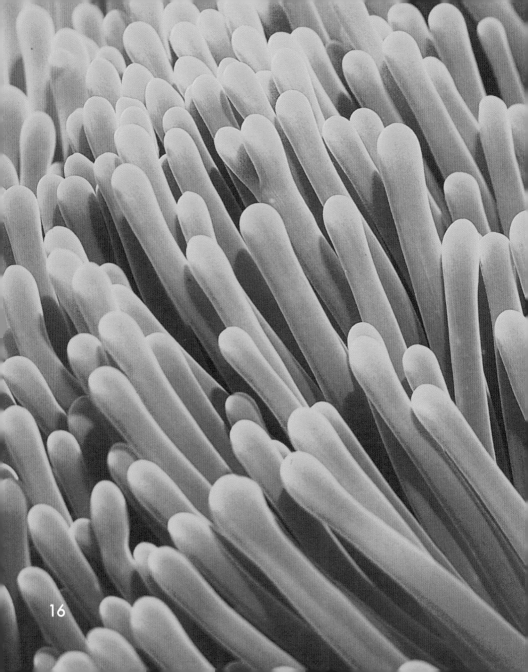

Sea anemones
have tentacles.

Sea anemones use their tentacles to sting prey.

Sea anemones use their tentacles to pull prey into the mouth.

Words to Know

attach—to join to something; sea anemones usually attach their bodies to rock or coral.

colorful—having many colors; sea anemone colors include blue, white, brown, red, and orange; some sea anemones are clear.

coral reef—an area of coral skeletons and rocks near the surface of the ocean

ocean—a large body of salt water

prey—an animal hunted by another animal for food; sea anemone prey include small ocean animals, fish, sea stars, and crabs.

sting—to hurt with a poisoned tip; sea anemones can sting prey with their tentacles.

tentacle—a long, flexible arm of an animal; sea anemones use their tentacles to sting prey.

Read More

Cerullo, Mary M. *Coral Reef: A City That Never Sleeps.* New York: Cobblehill Books, 1996.

Kalman, Bobbie. *A—B—Sea.* Crabapples. New York: Crabtree Publishing, 1995.

Smith, Sue. *Exploring Saltwater Habitats.* Mondo's Exploring Series. Greenvale, N.Y.: Mondo Publishing, 1994.

Internet Sites

Do you want to find out more about sea anemones? Let FactHound, our fact-finding hound dog, do the research for you.

Here's how:

1) Visit *http://www.facthound.com*

2) Type in the **Book ID** number: 0736802487

3) Click on **FETCH IT**.

FactHound will fetch Internet sites picked by our editors just for you!

Index/Word List

Word Count: 58
Early-Intervention Level: 12

Editorial Credits
Martha E. Hillman, editor; Steve Christensen, cover designer and illustrator; Kimberly Danger and Sheri Gosewisch, photo researchers

Photo Credits
Craig D. Wood, 1
Dembinsky Photo Assoc. Inc./Marilyn Kazmers, 4
Jay Ireland & Georgienne Bradley, cover, 6, 14, 20
Larry Tackett/Tom Stack & Associates, 16
Mo Yung Productions/Norbert Wu, 18
PhotoBank, Inc./Cranston, 8
Randy Morse/Tom Stack & Associates, 12
Robert E. Barber, 10